Trumpets
from the Islands of their
Eviction

Bilingual Press/Editorial Bilingüe

General Editor
Gary D. Keller

Managing Editor
Karen S. Van Hooft

Senior Editor
Mary M. Keller

Assistant Editor
David C. Rubí D.

Editorial Board
Juan Goytisolo
Francisco Jiménez
Eduardo Rivera
Severo Sarduy
Mario Vargas Llosa

Address
Bilingual Review/Press
Hispanic Research Center
Arizona State University
Tempe, Arizona 85287
(602) 965-3867

Trumpets
from the Islands of their
Eviction

Martín Espada

Bilingual Press/Editorial Bilingüe
TEMPE, ARIZONA

ISBN: 0-916950-72-7

Library of Congress Catalog Card Number: 87-71581

PRINTED IN THE UNITED STATES OF AMERICA

Front cover photograph, "Rosa Santiago: Returned Migrant,
Barrio La Pica, Maunabo, Puerto Rico," by Frank Espada,
Puerto Rican Diaspora Documentary Project, San Francisco,
California.

Back cover photograph of Martín Espada by Sam Cornish.

Cover design by Christopher J. Bidlack

Acknowledgments

This volume is supported by a grant from the National Endowment
for the Arts in Washington, D.C., a federal agency.

Song lyrics quoted in the poem, "Inmate Torres Sings Waiting for the
Parole Board" (page 60) are excerpted from "Pedro Navaja" by Ruben
Blades, copyright 1978 Ruben Blades Productions, Inc. Used by per-
mission.

Some of these poems have appeared or will appear in the following
periodicals and anthologies:

Abraxas (#25/26, May 1982), *The Bilingual Review/La Revista Bilin-
güe* (Vol. 9, No. 2, May-August 1982), *The Bloomsbury Review* (Vol. 5,
No. 7, April 1985), *The Greenfield Review* (Vol. 12, Nos. 1 and 2,
Summer/Fall 1984), *Hanging Loose* (#49, September 1986), *Imagine*
(Vol. 1, No. 2, Winter 1984), *The Jump River Review* (#11, Spring 1982),
Pinchpenny (Vol. 6, No. 1, April 1985), *Revista Chicano-Riqueña* (Vol.
7, No. 2, Summer 1984), *River Styx* (forthcoming 1987), *Signal* (forth-
coming, 1987), *Tonantzin* (Vol. 3, No. 1, November 1985), *A Confluence
of Colors* (Blue Reed Arts Press, 1984), and *Wire in the Blood* (Abraxas
Press, 1982).

CONTENTS

III. Pinball Between Madhouses

Many thanks to those who have supported and inspired me during the years these poems were written: Sam Cornish, Robert Creeley, Frank Espada, Luis Garden, Katherine Gilbert, June Jordan, Camilo Pérez, Andrew Salkey, and Clemente Soto Vélez.

A la memoria de mi abuelo
Francisco Espada Marrero
1892–1982

FOREWORD

Robert Creeley

The common disposition toward poetry has been long schooled by determinations of privilege and similar academic investment. So taught, it colonizes in the strictest of senses, patronizing its hosts, exploiting the common ground of human feeling for isolating details of style or taste. So again in school we learned of its difficulties only, the oblique reference of its superior information, the presumptive authority of its diffident gestures. Thus qualified, poetry became a markedly foreign world, both alien and alienating, and we were rarely if ever its people. It would not speak to us and we were finally ignorant of its ironic language.

But the actual world, thankfully, is one in which a plurality of poetries exist—not simply this one, or any such *one*, but many. The poet William Carlos Williams puts it most compactly: "Therefore each speech having its own character the poetry it engenders will be peculiar to that speech also in its own intrinsic form. . . ." Whitman had said that to have great poets, one needed great audiences—those who might hear intimately, intensely, the common voice in the singular person. The point is that this art can never leave the common body of its own communal life. It is not an *I* but "the wind that blows through me," as D. H. Lawrence has written.

Martín Espada is a poet of great communal power and he is also, with equal resource, the voice of intensive isolation. He says, for example, that he began to write as an adolescent because "nothing matched me." Small wonder that he felt so when one recognizes that after his family leaves the projects in Brooklyn— he is then about thirteen—their various locations (Valley Stream, Long Island, several towns in Maryland) are far removed from the communal habits of their Brooklyn neighborhood, whatever its limits had been. Racism becomes an insistent qualification and response insofar as these new communities are instance of "White Flight," i.e., a social migration of the period formed by those wishing to maintain a racial privilege. In these malignant camps of entrenched prejudice, Espada feels "less and less in touch."

So, expectably, Espada says that it is the resulting sense of dislocation that moves him to write, but he also proposes that this experience of being an outcast is literally the determinant in all Puerto Rican immigrant life. It's an old saying that a Puerto Rican spends more time in the air than on the ground. Harshly, complexly, "The Spanish of Our Out-Loud Dreams" makes clear with consummate tenderness the irrevocable transitions, seemingly without end:

> . . . Last night you cried,
> your black eyes shimmering darker
> than the room
> where we tried to sleep,
> crying like your father cried
> when you pulled away
> from the hospital bed,
> and for all the nights
> we have wandered with stuffed bags,
> not staying long enough
> to learn the language . . .

As he said of this poem, it is the insistent theme of migration, "The Spanish, etc. The third verse is really what it's all about."

The book's title poem is, of course, the complement, the "islands," the places left, or that one is going to, or has come to, or is leaving. He says wryly, "We're always being evicted. The 'trumpets' are our resistance to that, through identity, or more actively."

He is by no means an old man—twenty-eight—and yet his life has been so many determining places. Like the University of Maryland, where courses in creative writing and modern poetry make clear that "whatever I'm writing, it's not this." He stops writing for three or four years, he says. He has no models at first. "I didn't know it had a name." Certainly not those offered— Yeats, Eliot, Crane, Stevens—if the active terms and reference of his experience are to be respected and used. Finally, when he's about twenty and living elsewhere, a friend, Luis Garden Acosta, gives him a copy of *Latin American Revolutionary Poetry* (edited by Roberto Márquez and printed bilingually) with Pedro Pietri's classic poem of Puerto Rican community, "Puerto Rican Obituary," facing Ernesto Cardenal's rehearsal of Somozan ·corruption, "Zero Hour." "And the spark was lit. . . ." The connection: "People can write about *substantial* subjects. . . ."

At this point the father, Frank Espada, is an intensive key, I think. One can see, in fact, the bridge his life makes as definition for his son's in the title poem but even more complexly in the poem on the grandfather's death, "El señor está muerto": "son's body huge with a father's life." In turn, it is the literal community and person of Frank Espada which so invests his own son's commitment. It is his father's family and relationships that preoccupy the son finally. His father is a gifted photographer with determined political address and some of his work appears as an active complement to the poems in Espada's first book, *The Immigrant Iceboy's Bolero* (1982). He makes the point that his poetry "is always about more than me" and that it insists on the *outside*, echoing emotionally, politically and esthetically determinants in the father's own life. He speaks of the fact that his father's photographs were "always on the wall" despite there being long periods of inactivity, and that he sees himself as a "black and white" poet, for whom the principal agencies are foregrounding and shadow.

There is also the sense of *advocacy*—it is such a pervasive voice in this writing!—that Espada has in so many ways engaged. Thinking again of those "determining places": as a student at the University of Wisconsin in Madison, his interests are history (this is the major for the BA he holds, and it contributes curious data, as he says, such as the fact that Douglas MacArthur and Carl Sandberg both served in the US Army in Puerto Rico), radio journalism (a three-part documentary made in 1982 from material gathered in Nicaragua and broadcast on National Public Radio and elsewhere is an early national advice of circumstances there), and film—ultimately too expensive. *And* poetry. His first reading is at a bar in Madison where he also works as a bouncer.

But the job of most significance would seem the one he falls into by chance while working as a clerk in the state mental health system. The lawyer who had been responsible for representing

the rights of patients leaves unexpectedly for a better job. So
Martín Espada becomes the whole Advocacy Pool, simply be-
cause there is no one else so trained or at all interested. He had
dropped out of college at this point, had just turned twenty—
and must have been in some common crisis as to what his own
life was finally to be. In any case, he "soon knew the statutes
cold," as he put it, "Chapter 51.61: The Patient's Bill of Rights."
    Again, *advocacy* is the crucial term—"speaking or writing in
support (of something)" as the dictionary defines it. But the
meaning is more active in Espada's own qualification: "persua-
sion, making the case, putting it in human terms, quoting direct-
ly from the people. . . ." He says of the poem "La tormenta" that
it's a translation in part from the young boy ("A boy with wide
ears / and one shirt, / he walked across Guatemala, / México and
Arizona to get here . . . He wants to be called Tony / in the
United States . . .") who was "quite mad. . . ." *La muerte es una
tormenta.* "I couldn't say that, only he could say that. . . ."
    As of this writing [April 1986] Martín Espada works as a
lawyer for the META project in Cambridge, an organization
involved with the legal context of civil rights for immigrants and
with bilingual education laws in particular. He also teaches poet-
ry to sixth, seventh and eighth graders at the Agassiz School in
Cambridge, a very different world indeed. No doubt it is poetry
itself he speaks in defense of—or simply makes real for the
beleaguered young. That he's a lawyer too must amaze them—
with a three piece suit! Perhaps he can save us all.
    Whatever their circumstances poets make a world, piece by
piece, as best they can. Those most able are most ample—like
Pablo Neruda, a particular hero of Espada's. When the distances
become inexorable, the language disjunct, the place and person
lost in meager time and circumstance, when all that's left is what
one can finally say of it (or anything), then painfully, particular-
ly, poets remember, put back together the broken fragments of
the dismembered community. It is the power and the glory of
their art. It is also why there is not one singularizing poetry but
rather a host of annealing and restoring poets, who are as related
to the people as ever the people might be, in turn, to them.
When one first hears the voice of Espada's poems, the deter-
mined dignity, the intense, quiet care, when the cadence of the

language makes a movement having no didactic metric, rather a pace, an undulation, a way of intent walking, or feeling, then one recognizes the presence of this power, which no one owns but some may and can have, as does he. One wishes him safe journey.

ITHACA, NEW YORK
APRIL 1986

I. Trumpets from the Islands of Their Eviction

The Spanish of Our Out-Loud Dreams

para Nora Elena Díaz

You took your father
from the Bronx hospital
where the radiation failed,
to an island hospital
surrounded by palm trees
and hallways of nurses
who understood the Spanish
of his out-loud dreams.
Their hands gestured
at the hopeless chart.

Los puertorriqueños are always looking
for a place to sleep:
not in the houses we scrape clean for others,
not in the migrant camps we leave
after the crop is busheled,
not on the buses blowing out their bad lungs
in the horseshoe curve of highways,
or on the beaches of an island
spiked with the picket fences of tall hotels.

Back in the Bronx
and you're packing again,
moving southwest.
Last night you cried,
your black eyes shimmering darker
than the room
where we tried to sleep,
crying like your father cried
when you pulled away
from the hospital bed,

and for all the nights
we have wandered with stuffed bags,
not staying long enough
to learn the language.
My hand slipped through the night-thicket
of your hair,
as if the circling of my fingers
could give you rest.

In Puerto Rico,
your father tries to still
the jumping memory
of a numbers runner,
trying to sleep
between hospital-white curtains.

Let him sleep
where I slept:
shining in your passionate blackness,
the vigil of your shimmering gaze.

Trumpets from the Islands of Their Eviction

At the bar two blocks away,
immigrants with Spanish mouths
hear trumpets
from the islands of their eviction.
The music swarms into the barrio
of a refugee's imagination,
along with predatory squad cars
and bullying handcuffs.

Their eviction:
like Mrs. Alfaro, evicted
when she trapped ten mice,
sealed them in plastic sandwich bags
and gifted them to the landlord;
like Daniel, the boy stockaded
in the back of retarded classrooms
for having no English
to comfort third-grade teachers;
like my father thirty-five years ago,
brown skin darker than the Air Force uniform
that could not save him, seven days county-jailed
for refusing the back of a Mississippi bus;
like the nameless Florida jíbaro
the grocery stores would not feed
in spite of the dollars he showed,
who returned with a machete,
collected cans from shelves
and forced the money
into the clerk's reluctant staring hand.

We are the ones identified by case number,
summons in the wrong language,
judgment without stay of execution.
Mrs. Alfaro has thirty days
to bundle the confusion of five children
down claustrophobic stairs
and away from the apartment.

And at the bar two blocks away,
immigrants with Spanish mouths
hear trumpets
from the islands of their eviction.
The sound scares away devils
like tropical fish
darting between the corals.

El señor está muerto

He was Paco the gambler,
Francisco the bookkeeper in three languages,
Papito the generous grandfather of Tres Reyes.
He was ninety years old,
his fluttering swelled hand
would pull the oxygen mask away,
and he howled all night for morphine,
for water he could not swallow.

Sporadic rain scattered on leaves and sheets of tin roof,
fragile shacks and trees leaning distant in hospital window.
His son and grandson passed shards of coffee-soaked bread,
one keeping vigil while the other did not sleep
on the mattress. The night was a dark
wounded animal, the scrape of forced breathing
and labored ribs heard from the corner.
Twice they yelled for morphine when the moans were too
                                                    strong,
then were told a man so weak would lose
the last palpitations of the heart with a painkilling drug.
In the morning, his eyes were white boats overturned,
blind yet amazed at hallucinations, at a sight
through the ceiling. An orderly greeted him
and squirted juice in the dry gaping mouth.

He kept living. Later that morning,
his son and grandson at the funeral business
surrounded by steel coffins docked in waiting,
a stranger from the next room called.
The hospital words were recited by telephone
with medical apology, then the son loudly reporting
"el señor está muerto"—the gentleman is dead—
son's body huge with a father's life
lowered to a leather chair.
He spoke: a plain coffin would be carried without religion
to Cementerio San Juan tomorrow afternoon.

Signing the burial papers, a sob struck the back of his head,
caught between the eyes with his fingers.

An uncle, a man once a priest eulogized,
"Francisco Espada era un hombre contento,
porque durante su vida tenía la oportunidad de dar:"
Francisco Espada was a contented man,
for during his life he had the opportunity to give.
Those who knew the giving, the serious children
of grandfather Papito, the old women mouths creased
with the remembered gifts of Paco the gambler
fifty years ago, all became the dark march
approaching a grave too fresh for the headstone.

The moist red earth was plowed aside, son and grandson
pallbearers for a coffin surprisingly light, gripping the rails
against a white sky that almost rained.

Mariano Explains Yanqui Colonialism
to Judge Collings

Judge: Does the prisoner understand his rights?
Interpreter: ¿Entiende usted sus derechos?
Prisoner: ¡Pa'l carajo!
Interpreter: Yes.

Where the Disappeared Would Dance

Ponce, Puerto Rico, 1985

The shoeshine man squats at the hotel door,
points and shouts at the walkers
scraping his pavement,
under cheap loudspeakers
distorting "¡baratísimo!"
from the discount store;
under the busy hands of the jobless,
jabbing with streetcorner talk.

Ponce: the plaza crooked with detours
and stopped construction,
cars hot and snorting with impatience.
Above the bright rough signs
that trade in dollars,
balconies are crust-fragile, shutters nailed,
and windows keep the stunned faces
that remember Spain.
Even the festivals now
wear factory-masks,
and anglo-american soldiers
stride through the parade crowd.

The labors of cement in Ponce
paid for a banker's art museum
and centuries of European painting.
No one from the plaza goes there,
but a man thin as disease,
in pava straw hat and a white suit
left by the dead to charity,
brags to the sandwich stand
that he knows the governor.

Away from the factory road,
aboriginal stones circle a field
where the disappeared would dance,

where god-carvings still listen
for songs of worship,
and wild grass thickens
over the skeletons of caciques.

A shallow blue light
drifts between mountains
with a minute of rain,
and the leaves of moriviví
are closing.

Operation Bootstrap: San Juan, 1985

Man with one crutch
staggering between lanes of traffic
begging coins
for the other crutch

David Leaves the Saints for Paterson

David's arm hung near-paralyzed
after the stabbing,
and there was no work in the coffee
of barrio Hills Brothers,
so he learned to smoke with the other hand
and plotted to leave Puerto Rico.

His mother sponge-washed the plaster santos
every week, draped statues crowded
with flowers. Then Tata, la abuela,
would nod with ceremony, foretelling
money and sickness, mouth quavering ajar
with the dialects of the many dead.
In spite of prophecy at Jardines del Paraíso
housing project, no one could stop drinking.

David left the saints for Paterson:
the boot factory, then a hospital job
wheeling carts of delicate bottles
through light-bleached corridors on late shift.

Together with his father at the Paterson hospital,
the gallo-man who learned to box in prison,
who also pushes the medicine carts to impatient doctors
and cannot stop drinking.

Toque de queda: Curfew in Lawrence

Lawrence, Massachusetts, August 1984

Now the archbishop comes to Lawrence
to say a Spanish mass.
But the congregation understands
without translation:
the hammering of the shoe factory,
sweating fever of infected August,
housing project's asylum chatter,
dice on the sidewalk,
saints at the window,
two days' murky pollution of riot-smoke,
the mayor's denials.

Toque de queda: curfew signs
outlaw the conspiracy of foreign voices
at night.
Barricades surround the buildings
widow-black from burning, collapsed in shock.
After the explosion of shotgun pellets
and shattered windshields,
sullen quiet stands watching on Tower Hill,
trash, brick and bottle fragments
where the arrested kneeled, hands clapped
to the neck, and bodies with Spanish names
slammed into squad cars, then disappeared.

The mobs are gone: white adolescents
who chanted USA and flung stones
at the scattering of astonished immigrants,
ruddy faces slowing the car to shout spick
and wave beer cans.

Now the archbishop comes to Lawrence
to say a Spanish mass.
At the housing project where they are kept,
they're collecting money for bail.

We Live by What We See at Night

for my father

When the mountains of Puerto Rico
flickered in your sleep
with a moist green light,
when you saw green bamboo hillsides
before waking to East Harlem rooftops
or Texas barracks,
when you crossed the bridge ·
built by your grandfather
over a river glimpsed
only in interrupted dreaming,
the craving for that island birthplace
burrowed, deep
as thirty years' exile,
constant as your pulse.

This was the inheritance
of your son, born in New York:
that years before
I saw Puerto Rico,
I saw the mountains
looming above the projects,
overwhelming Brooklyn,
living by what I saw at night,
with my eyes closed.

Tony Went to the Bodega but He Didn't Buy Anything

para Angel Guadalupe

Tony's father left the family
and the Long Island city projects,
leaving a mongrel-skinny puertorriqueño boy
nine years old
who had to find work.

Makengo the Cuban
let him work at the bodega.
In grocery aisles
he learned the steps of the dry-mop mambo,
banging the cash register
like piano percussion
in the spotlight of Machito's orchestra,
polite with the abuelas who bought on credit,
practicing the grin on customers
he'd seen Makengo grin
with his bad yellow teeth.

Tony left the projects too,
with a scholarship for law school.
But he cursed the cold primavera
in Boston;
the cooking of his neighbors
left no smell in the hallway,
and no one spoke Spanish
(not even the radio).

So Tony walked without a map
through the city,
a landscape of hostile condominiums
and the darkness of white faces,
sidewalk-searcher lost
till he discovered the projects.

Tony went to the bodega
but he didn't buy anything:
he sat by the doorway satisfied
to watch la gente (people
island-brown as him)
crowd in and out,
hablando español,
thought: this is beautiful,
and grinned
his bodega grin.

This is a rice and beans
success story:
today Tony lives on Tremont Street,
above the bodega.

Tiburón

East 116th
and a long red car
stalled with the hood up
roaring salsa
like a prize shark
mouth yanked open
and down in the stomach
the radio
of the last fisherman
still tuned
to his lucky station

Los Sures

Williamsburg, Brooklyn, Winter 1984

The bright-color portrait of Jesus jumps
on South 4th Street plaster
where the subway train's iron tremor
startles like the hunger that wakes us,
night in Los Sures
shake your black hair down,
and the night is a woman's darkness.

Night is the only tenant left,
night is the face at every window,
where yellowish heat splashed soot on walls,
spit a mouthful of glass
onto South 4th Street sidewalk,
night in Los Sures
shake your black hair down,
leaning on the ruined grain of brick.

But the builders have a defiant blueprint,
the hammer's tap multiplies furious
as the hands of plena drummers,
the abandoned church will be a health center,
the evacuated buildings on South 4th Street
will shout with the voices of the living,
night in Los Sures
shake your black hair down,
you are a dark woman rising,
turning hips and heartbeat quick.

From an Island You Cannot Name

Thirty years ago,
your linen-gowned father stood
in the dayroom of the VA hospital,
grabbing at the plastic
identification bracelet
marked Negro,
shouting "I'm not!
Take it off!
I'm Other!"

The army photograph
pinned to your mirror
says he was,
black, Negro,
dark as West Indian rum.

And this morning,
daughter of a man
from an island you cannot name,
you gasp tears
trying to explain
that you're Other,
that you're not.

The Chota and the Patrón

The tennis players flitted
with the ball's echo
over the spotlit court,
next to the grower's house
big and white as the moon
in Delaware night.
Down a path of summer mud,
Spanish glimmered
in the straining brown light
of laborers' barracks.

The car from Legal Aid
growled quietly with headlights off,
trespassing, past the tennis courts
and down to the barracks.
There the men from Yauco, Utuado, Humacao,
who left Puerto Rico
with their migrants' hungry faith
in promises and rumors, rose from cots
too narrow for sleep, the clack
of domino games and cheap radio buzz,
crowding each other to speak,
men illiterate but for their hands and backs
browned and reddened by the overseer sun
which followed close behind
in the fields of green pepper.
They shouted and their coarse hands trembled:
cool coffee and charred beans
at mealtime,
the drowned latrines covered with planks
that leaked in a frenzy of green flies,
the thin envelope of dollars
counted in curses every week.

A human face
crushed against the screen door
watching, remembering,

glaring like a wary scavenger
through the wire.
Noticed, the face snapped away,
startled back into the darkness
where it hid.
The others grinned and sneered:
"chota," they said.
A suckling goat. An informer,
stumbling through the mud now
to the tennis court.

Next week, the car from Legal Aid,
headlights off,
skimmed beneath the surface of the night
down to the barracks.
The room shuffled
with the stunned repetition of chores,
the turn of avoiding stares
and threatened quiet leaning on the cots.
No one signed court papers.
Swinging the screen door open,
a smooth-faced mulato boy
mumbled about the chota
and the patrón,
apologizing for the fright
that worms like a parasite
through the bloodstream and intestines
of laborers,
visions of exile to the unemployment office
and a boarding house in the city,
or the crewleader's gun butt
protruding from his pants.

The car from Legal Aid dragged away.
Inside the barracks, the raw backs
hunched over domino games and beer bottles
in grim concentration,
men auctioned to the fields
where dark skin grows darker
in the poisonous heat.

Voodoo Cucumbers

He was Haitian too,
but he was Doc Hunt's crewleader:
everybody called him 99
because he kept the Haitian crews
working with voodoo power,
picking Maryland crops hands adrenalin-driven
by 99 double-number bad magic.

They wouldn't leave without him.
The Haitian crews, some marooned
by the shipwreck of used cars
paid for with no English
in the next town,
others shouting and slamming dominoes
on the common table,
betting postponed wages
in front of the satan-hot metal shacks.
Immigration papers say
Entry Without Inspection,
Deportable.
Two weeks gone
waiting for work,
waiting for 99,
they could pick peaches west of here.
They won't leave without him.

This is Doc Hunt's trade:
99's crews pick voodoo cucumbers
and cursed tomatoes
weathered at roadside stands,
cellophaned at supermarkets,
sold for salad.

Water, White Cotton, and the Rich Man

Rosa's body stopped growing
at the age of twelve.
Ten hours a day
blurred pesticide and sweat,
squeezed headaches and full bladder
surrounded by widening white-cotton sun,
doing what Mexicanos in Lubbock, Texas
did for working.

So she worked,
beside her quiet father
(father with thousands of cotton field days
lost in the dry riverbeds
of his hands),
floating with him in a scorched white dream
of places distant from the black tar
of the county trunk;
soon the jug was empty,
and every time Rosa swallowed
she felt the scraping in her neck
that reminded her of water.
Twelve years old, the child watched the road
and imagined a rich man
driving a silver car
that meandered through the cotton fields
to bring her water, chilled
in a long bright glass,
close enough to see
the moisture-beads evaporate.

She learned her thirst, slowly,
over the days that no landlord
volunteered the drippings of his tap,
a closing throat, paste of saliva
and humidity that becomes rage;

twenty years after
her body stopped growing
Rosa keeps a peasant daughter's hallucination
still hidden,
feels it scratching every time
her throat is dry.

The Right Hand of a Mexican Farmworker in Somerset County, Maryland

A rosary tattoo
between thumb
and forefinger
means that
every handful
of crops and dirt
is a prayer,
means that Christ
had hard hands
too

II. La tormenta

The Jeep Driver

For Fernando Reñazco, Nicaragua, July 1982

"I know everyone
in this country,"
he says,
"even the devil."
His indio face flattens
when he laughs,
cursing the gringos
or pumping his fists
as he steers
a remembered machinegun.

Fernando's smile
is not revenge against dead patrones;
he smiles like a tired man
who's had a chance to rest.
For years of his life
the coal mines glistened blackly,
and sugar cane bristled
in Nicaragüense summer,
through generations of parading military,
mutilated dissidents sunken at Laguna Masaya.
Fernando's face has no expression,
remembering a tall boy
swinging at coal-rock and cane-stalk
(a father's death is work),
or driving a truck ponderous
over the dirt roads,
starved throats of the Americas.
He learned a song then
about rain and houses of cardboard;
he still sings it.

When the rebellion began,
Fernando from the doorway watched
the hurried carrying
of dangle-limbed bodies
to the burning.
But the soldiers grabbed
even the watchers in doorways.

So he became a combatiente,
jeep driver for the rebels,
legs paralyzed after thirty days'
fighting through floodwaters at the knee—
chorus of water, percussion of rifle shot—
he healed, walked again, swiveled the jeep
plane-hunted on the last retreat from Masaya,
then celebration in crowd-crazy Managua
when the dictator was finally gone
to the sky.

Now he drives with us through Zelaya, the north,
telling us he is still indio puro de Monimbó,
bragging of the Nicaragüense Flor de Caña rum
he will not drink himself.
Jeep driver for the ministry of land reform:
driving through the mountain roads,
rough dry throats of the Americas,
between crater-valleys and shallow rivers
and red malinche flowers
exploded by Mayan gods in the act of dying,
Fernando's hand spreads wide from the rattling jeep,
striking the wind,
sweeping the wind.

Again the Mercenaries: Atlantic Coast of Nicaragua, 4th of July 1982

The Río Sucio drags the reaching brown hand of branches
away from a shoreline of trees,
current quickened like the pulse of furious veins
spreading darkness over the cocodrilo's rough back.
Here dusk is a mulato, night the grandson
of a slave, walking the river into mines
collapsed like the caverns of an exhausted lung.
"The whites took the gold and left tuberculosis,"
says el indio, maneuvering the jeep,
and again the mercenaries
have gathered their muddy shadows close to the river,
paid with the rifles and lead of a distant monarch.

From this nameless road a truck is thrown,
side-sprawled, underbelly still warm iron,
and approaching three unknown men swaggering machetes.

Grito for Nicaragua

para Mauricio y barrio René Cisneros, Managua

After years of land stripped brown and humiliated as a
                                                    slave's back,
after the living flailed by the Guardia into crematorium-
                                                    volcanoes,
the corpses dragged through funeral-slow clouded rivers,
after tree-hidden boys trembled quickly in the waiting of
                                                    ambush,
the first killed soldier and vomiting in the humid secrecy of
                                                    night,
after rifles kicking again with the force of slaughtered cousins,
after airlift evacuation of the general's family over caving city
                                                    walls:

the shacks grow on stripped land, resurrection of planks,
the unsteady spine of nails, wounds grafted with cardboard
                                                    patch,
the dark backs pushing together, becoming one back to lift
                                                    long pipe,
the shovel's iron hungry for the dirt of latrine digging;

then the remains of shacks and fields charred by raiders
will be raised again in the arms of those left unburned,
then invading squadrons will struggle with the weight
of ammunition in the river's churning,
then mercenaries and military advisors
will sleep in the rain of border patrol snipers,
then their bone fragments will be strewn like smashed pottery
with the dwindling reminder of their stench
for the curiosity of flies and children.

La tormenta

"La muerte es una tormenta.
Death is a storm,"
he said.
"And the village
is an anthill scattering."
Héctor in the army
of El Salvador:
conscripted at fourteen,
a deserter three years later.

A boy with wide ears
and one shirt,
he walked across Guatemala,
México and Arizona to get here,
almost swallowing
too much river and mud
at the border.
He wants to be called Tony
in the United States.

In the basement,
part way through
translated instructions
on where he will eat today,
Tony pulls the hood
of a big borrowed coat
over his head and bodyrocks,
a monk shadowboxing
at the clang of churchbells,
moving to a song
with a distant helicopter beat,
la tormenta
and the anthill scattering.

Green and Red, Verde y Rojo

for Jacobo Mena

At night, when Beacon Hill
is a private army
of antique gas lamps
glowing in single file,
Jacobo vacuum-cleans
the law office of Adams and Blinn,
established 1856, with the founder's
wire-rimmed Protestant face
still supervising the labor,
a restored photograph in the window.

Jacobo's face
is indio-guatemalteco,
bored as the work,
round as worry,
heavy as waiting.
Guatemala is green and red,
green volcanoes, red birds,
green like rivers in rain,
red like coffee beans at harvest,
the river-green and quetzal bird-red
of his paintings,
perfiles del silencio.

Testimony of death-squad threats
by telephone, shrilled in the dark,
the flash of fear's adrenaline,
and family stolen with the military's greed
for bodies, all recorded by stenographers,
then dismissed:
Guatemala leaves no proof,
and immigration judges are suspicious
only of the witnesses, who stagger and crawl
through America. Asylum denied,
appeal pending.

As he waits, Jacobo paints
in green and red, verde y rojo,
and at night he cleans the office
of Adams and Blinn,
where Guatemala cannot be felt
by the arrogant handshake of lawyers,
where there is no green or red,
only his shadow blending
with the other shadows in the room,
and all the hours of the night
to picture the executioners.

The Firing Squad Is Singing in Chile

It was years ago,
at the moment of the coup,
that the military arrested
Víctor Jara,
alleged communist, a singer;

they took him to the stadium,
where thousands of the suspected stood
waiting for a bullet,
where skulls leaked
in interrogation rooms
like earthenware pots
spilling their wine.

He sang for them,
and they, neckbruised,
heartbeat drumming
in the forehead,
fear-eyed they,
they sang.

And he sang,
sang after the gun butts
fractured his hands
to stop the guitar,
sang though they pried the tongue
from his head
so that a mouth-cavern of red
was his song,
sang till the guards
pointed metallic snouts
and punctured his chest
with machineguns' iron insect sting.

There were thousands,
and each one
had a wake in the mouth
for a dead singer,

a quiet between sorrowful teeth
for a mutilated song.

And the military made laws.
They banned the songs,
Laborer's Prayer
and the Child of the Plow,
Winds of the People
and Song to the Fallen,
documents stamped subversive
in the hundreds.

They banned
the armadillo-shell charango,
the quena flute
and its condor-god throat,
the bombo drum
of mapuche ritual,
infected by communists,
incinerated subversive.

They banned the mention
of Víctor Jara's name,
a repented subversive.

These are the junta's policies:

bureaucrats proofreading
music sheets,
police escorting those
who mispronounce their lyrics
to shock batons and spotlights
in a humid room.

The army, in twos and threes
on street corners,
leaning on rifles,
a vigil of cigarettes,
listening
for years.

And years later,
exiles in cafes sing,
smuggled tape recordings sing,
night watchmen late in warehouses sing,
labor camp prisoners anally raped cry and sing,
the wives and mothers of the disappeared in protest sing,
guerrilleros assembling rifles in a clandestine basement sing,
as if a butchered tongue
could stop Chile from singing.

Generals, constipated with blood,
are overhearing it:

the condemned in a row
are singing, singing
with the furious chorus
of the firing squad.

Manuel Is Quiet Sometimes

He was quiet again,
driving east on 113,
near the slaughterhouse
on the day after Christmas,
not mourning,
but almost bowed,
like it is after the funeral
of a distant relative,
thoughtful,
sorrow on the border at dusk.

Vietnam was a secret.
Some men there collected ears,
some gold teeth.
Manuel collected the moist silences
between bursts of mortar.
He would not tell
what creatures laughed in his sleep,
or what blood was still drying
from bright to dark
in moments of boredom
and waiting.
A few people knew
about the wound,
a jabbing in his leg
(though he refused
to limp);
I knew about the time
he went AWOL.

Driving east on 113,
he talked
about how he keeps
the car running
in winter. It's
a good car,
he said.

There was the brief illumination
of passing headlights,
and slaughterhouse smoke
halted in the sky.

Another night,
the night of the Chicano dance,
Manuel's head swung slow and lazy
with drinking.
He smiled repeatedly,
a polite amnesiac,
and drank other people's beer,
waiting for the dancers
to leave their tables
so he could steal the residue
in plastic cups.
It was almost 2 AM
when he toppled,
aimless as something beheaded,
collapsing so he huddled
a prisoner on the floor.

The shell of his body
swung elbows
when we pulled him up.
He saw me first,
seeing a stranger.
His eyes were the color
of etherized dreams,
eyes that could
castrate the enemy,
easy murder watching me
with no reflection.

This is what he said:
"I never lied
to you, man."

Boot Camp Incantation

Marine base, Quantico, Virginia, 1977

What does a Marine feel
when he kills the enemy?

The recoil of his M-16.

III. Pinball Between Madhouses

Leo Blue's and the Tiger Rose

Mitchell walked three miles
for cigarettes
and a telephone call to Legal Aid:
take me away from Leo Blue's,
he said.

Labor camp: tin shacks and a sand pit,
gathering place for apparitions
killed by the heat;
through the tin surface and screens
the sun crawls like a bright spider
that startles the eyes and heart,
a sweat-demon slowly walking.

This is a row of darkskinned men
with old shoes,
recruited from the mission shelter
in Tampa, drink-poisoned then,
still blurred:
a swallow of Tiger Rose wine
before cucumber picking
in the swollen light of morning.
They dump cucumber buckets
for another taking
of the craved wine
from a crewleader's truck.

All day bending
like something storm-broken
and left to sway,
dream scarecrows
with stiff hands picking.
Ten hours gone.

Return to camp,
back to the crewleader's gospel music tapes
loudly preaching,
minimum wage signs no one can read
posted in the kitchen,
camp meals of pigs' ears and pinto beans
deducted with brown pay-envelope arithmetic:
Mitchell works three days
for six dollars.
We wait
as he soaps the farmer's car
to pay for the last
of his meals.

We leave the brilliance of sharp-angled roof,
old shoes unclaimed
near hunchback mattress.

Pinball Between Madhouses

Slum building in blurred sun
and a woman started shrieking
on the sixth floor.
Hospital men, white men
with tightened faces
strapped her to a stretcher.

The crowd was a jury of staring,
watching her loaded
through ambulance doors
and the red light floating.

The ambulance left, bright and loud
like a traveling circus,
a pinball between madhouses.

My grandfather
was in the madhouse too.
His hands shook
as if possessed
by the spirit
of a drowned ragtime piano player.

I worked in such a place,
of painted windows,
blocks of clean paper,
and the sad chant of machines.

We were a printing plant
and printed the *Military Digest*
and did not talk.

Drugs in the Forehead

Iron doors, windows sunken and repeating themselves
in sterilized corridors, fluorescent lights
and mopped floors spotted in a dream state,
scrubfleshed hand dutifully keeping the logbook;
dayroom, used furniture in the corner,
television's image greying and dumb,
a coffee cup, the ward tilted to the angle
of slouched men, between every bored cigarette
a face with drugs in the forehead.

Majeski Plays the Saxophone

"He killed his parents
and buried them
in the city dump,"
the Treatment Director said,
white-haired keeper
of crazy house folklore
in the file cabinet.

Majeski plays the saxophone
down in mental hospital's
abandoned bowling alley,
devils tattooed on his arms,
headshaking overgrown hair and beard
with the murmur of the trembled horn,
bodyrocking to saxophone's
drugged confession.

Social workers caucused,
doctors conferred:
"We don't know
what's wrong with him,"
said one.
"He's a sociopath,"
said another.
"Plays the goddamn saxophone,"
said another.

And Majeski plays the saxophone,
saxophone like a deaf-mute moaning,
like a fugitive's hoarse breathing,
blues from a radio
at the cemetery, posthumous 78
repeating the town secret.

"He's here for the rest of his life,"
the Treatment Director said,

and had to smile
when he said it.
On the ward,
the guards played poker
and squabbled with the patients
over the TV.

Majeski plays the saxophone,
ballad moist and bitter
as the taste of tongue's blood,
swinging slow welled trachea-hot
and forced out the mouth,
jazz.

Eight Hundred A.D. on the Ward

An observation patient
wailing through
the night watchman's sleep
is only remembering
a Gregorian chant
from the monastery
he visits in dreams

Transient Hotel Werewolf

At the desk he asked
where the pay phone was,
then stumbled on the stairway landing,
wheeled and pounced
on the lobby tile,
snarling and snapping
at a tail that wasn't there,
transient hotel werewolf
spinning frantic circles
on his knees.

Later, after the hospital,
he paced the lobby,
quiet but hair torn
with a rage he did not remember.
And Pablo, who hours ago
calmed him enough for the ambulance,
kept saying:
"It wasn't like he ran out
of medication.
It was just that
he was afraid
he would run out."

So there was no full moon
or a family curse
that grew the tail
on a werewolf tonight;
only the chemicals
baying in his brain.

Inmate Torres Sings Waiting for the Parole Board

For inmate Torres
the dominoes never matched,
the numbers he never hit
stenciled across blue
prison-issue denim.

"Sí, soy puertorriqueño también.
From Roxbury," he says in the hallway,
grinning and scratching a beard
he's too young to grow.
"I needed money,
got crazy,
took a gun and held up a guy.
And the guy was a judge."
He grins again, funny the bad
dropout arithmetic of a ten-year sentence.

Now, waiting for the parole board,
inmate Torres tries to believe
in his own strut.
The last inmate returns from the hearing room,
chained and laughing with grief.
And inmate Torres sings:
"La vida te da sorpresas,
sorpresas te da la vida,
ay Dios."

Some people still sing
when they pray,
and inmate Torres
sings for a surprise.

The Policeman's Ball

It was
a policeman's ball,
old-timey cop stomp
polka kept the beat
with a boot blood-spotted
and a hand that clapped,
so that after the dance
the suspect couldn't
snap his fingers

Job Search Got Us Down

In the waiting room
I read the job ads
to impress
the social worker
when he calls my name

A man curses and flings
the welfare form
at the ceiling
because intake says
he can't prove
that he has no address

A sign with big letters
and a small phone number
says:
JOB SEARCH
GOT YOU DOWN?

Watch Me Swing

I was the fifth man hired
for the city welfare cleaning crew
at the old Paterson Street ballpark,
Class A minor leagues.
Opening Day was over,
and we raked the wooden benches
for the droppings of the crowd:
wrappers, spilled cups, scorecards,
popcorn cartons, chewed and spit hot dogs,
a whiskey bottle, a condom dried on newspaper.

We swung our brooms,
pausing to watch home runs sail
through April imagination
over the stone fence three hundred feet away,
baseball cracking off the paint factory sign
across Washington Street.
We shuffled and kicked,
plowed and pushed
through the clinging garbage,
savoring our minimum wages.

When the sweeping was done,
and the grandstand benches
clean as Sunday morning pews,
the team business manager
inspected the aisles,
reviewed the cleaning crew
standing like broomstick cadets
and said:
"We only need four."
I was the fifth man hired.

As the business manager
strode across the outfield
back to his office,

I wanted to leap the railing,
crouch at home plate
and swing my broom,
aiming a smacked baseball
for the back of his head,
yelling, "watch me swing, boss,
watch me swing."

Confession of the Tenant in Apartment #2

The landlord's
beige Fleetwood Cadillac
died in front of the building,

and I was secretly happy
that my jumper cables
didn't work

The Moon Shatters on Alabama Avenue

A wooden box rattled
with coins for the family,
on a stoop where the roots
of a brown bloodstain grew.

Brooklyn, 1966: Agropino Bonillo was his name,
a neighbor, the yellow leaflet said,
a kitchen worker who walked home
under the scaffolding of the trains at night,
hurrying past streetlamps with dark eyes.
He was there when the boys surrounded him,
quick with shouts and pushing,
addiction's hunger in a circle.
When he had no money,
the kicking began.

The mourners clustered at the storefront,
then marched between cadaverous buildings
down Alabama Avenue,
as the night turned blue with rain
in a heavy sky of elevated track.
The first candles struggled, smothered wet;
onlookers leaned warily as they watched.
A community of faces gathered and murmured
in the dim circles of light,
kept alive by cupped hands.

In the asphalt street shined black from rain
and windows where no one was seen
hesitant candles appeared, a pale blur started
on the second floor, another trembling glimmer
slipped to the back of the march, then more,
multiplied into a constellation
spreading over the sidewalk,
a swarm of candles that throbbed descending
tenement steps in the no longer absolute dark,

as if the moon had shattered
and dropped in burning white pieces
on the night.

His name was Agropino Bonillo,
spoken remembering
every sixty-dollar week
he was bent in the kitchen,
his children
who could not dress for winter
and brawled against welfare taunts
at the schoolyard,
the unlit night
that the sweep of legs was stopped
by his belly and his head.

And the grief of thousands illuminated city blocks,
moving with the tired feet of the poor:
candles a reminder of the wakes too many and too soon,
the frustrated prayers and pleading with saints,
in memoriam for generations of sacrificed blood
warm as the wax sticking to their fingers,
and years of broken streetlamps, bowed
with dark eyes, where addiction's hunger waits nervously.

Over the wooden box, a woman's face
was slick in a drizzle of tears.
Her hand dropped coins like seed.

DANCING TO THE MUSIC OF
AN "OTHER" VOICE: MARTIN ESPADA

Diana L. Vélez

Trumpets from the Islands of Their Eviction is Martín Espada's second collection of poems. His earlier *The Immigrant Iceboy's Bolero*, seventeen poems intercalated with his father's fine photographs of the Puerto Rican diaspora, is a gem now in its third printing.[1]

This new title, like that of the earlier book, indexes the double inscription of the text: there is music here, trumpets of a salsa riff, triumphal trumpets; but there is also a multiplicity of isolations—islands. And finally there is power—the wrong end of it—eviction.

Such is our entry into a rich discourse.

It is always exciting to find the work of a gifted new writer. But one should exercise caution here. These poems must be read slowly; each verse, each syllable should be savored, given its due. There is a multiplicity of meanings here that requires a free play of signification.

There is thematic variety as well: some of the poems are openly political metaphors of struggle. The first section celebrates the people Pedro Pietri wished "had kept their eyes open at the funeral of their fellow employees who came to this country to make a fortune and were buried without underwears."[2] Other poems in this first section are about workers in migrant camps, the abuses to which they are subject as a condition of their employment and their multiform resistances ("Water, White Cotton, and the Rich Man," "Voodoo Cucumbers").

Espada's trip to Central America a few years ago gave him rich material for the second section, entitled "La tormenta," which is about the poverty as well as the resistance of the Nicara-

guan people in the face of oppression and the toll which the
United States' undeclared war in the region is taking on them.

Some of the pieces are humorous while still others are haunt-
ingly lyrical, even disturbing. There are some flaws, but it is clear
from even a cursory reading that Martín Espada has a rare
poetic gift, a gift recognized by the National Endowment for the
Arts this year when they awarded him a fellowship so that he can
continue to write poetry.

Background

Before further discussing the poems I will begin to place this
collection in its socio-historical and literary contexts.

As the title of this collection of poems indicates, Puerto Ri-
cans are a people evicted: evicted from an island in droves in the
nineteen fifties by a development program called Operation
Bootstrap, an important component of which was massive emi-
gration of what planners called "excess population" to the Unit-
ed States mainland as a way of reducing unemployment figures.
These government planners, both Puerto Rican and North
American, could then celebrate the economic miracle of an in-
dustrialized, "modernized" Puerto Rico that had solved its pov-
erty problem in one generation.

So droves of Puerto Ricans left the island, but on the main-
land their problems did not end. Many suffered eviction once
again, this time because of urban renewal, the gentrification of
neighborhoods, or because slumlords wanted to collect on insur-
ance policies. (This is the theme of "Mrs. Báez Serves Coffee on
the Third Floor" in *The Immigrant Iceboy's Bolero*).

If they manage to realize their dream of a return to la Isla,
Puerto Ricans suffer exclusion once more, for there the space
has been invaded by United States capital. Those who do return
are no longer at ease on "the beaches of an island spiked with the
picket fences of tall hotels" ("The Spanish of Our Out Loud
Dreams").

The four "moments" in the coming-to-consciousness of the
Puerto Rican outlined by Juan Flores—the here-and-now, Puer-
to Rican Background, re-entry and branching out—give this col-
lection of poems its internal logic and structure as the poetic
persona moves through the spaces—temporal, spatial, imagi-

nary—that define a people in the process of becoming conscious social subjects.[3]

Context

There is no small measure of irony to be savored in reading this book manuscript in 1986, the year of the Statue of Liberty celebration. A bell sounds—the signal to celebrate America—and the Pavlovian creatures are off. The journalists, the modern-day mythmakers, the high priests of mass culture artifacts give us Miss Liberty hats while members of the nation's intellectual elite discuss the cultural, racial and ethnic pluralism that has been the official signature of North America's creed in this century.

But there are a number of gaps in this official narrative, a narrative reproduced at an alarming rate.

The first gap, one which lets us start to deconstruct that smooth uniformity of vision, is the most obvious one: today's immigrants. This includes Haitian boat people and Central American refugees. It includes emigrés and Latin American political refugees fleeing political persecution, a persecution too often facilitated by United States aid to repressive regimes back home. As the celebratory Miss Liberty discourses multiply, some of us observe that today the poor, the tired, the hungry cannot count on this country's government to protect them unless it is politically expedient to do so. So they turn instead to courageous allies in the Sanctuary movement, clerics and lay people alike who risk jail to defend those labeled by the Administration as "economic refugees." Today, as during the slave period, what we should celebrate is not official doctrine but the country's oppositional voices—the Sanctuary movement's underground railroad. Those are the voices which now refuse the injustice, the barbarism of the State.

This hard work of resistance was taking place while Fourth of July festival planners worried about how to fit in all those vendors and movable toilets. And in stage rear of this movable feast we discern the countenance of President Reagan inexorably dismantling the welfare state. Against this overarching backdrop, the country's so-called minorities know that America's latent nativism is now back full force and with a vengeance. Verbal attacks on the society's Other have become an acceptable form of public discourse, statue or no statue.

This takes us to the other gap in the official story of America as a nation of immigrants, this society's refused Other: Asians, Blacks, Chicanos, Native Americans, Puerto Ricans—the so-called non-whites. Ironically, Chicanos and Native Americans are perhaps *too* American—but many members of the dominant culture see these groups and the others mentioned as not quite American enough. They are the lumps that never quite melted into that pot so familiar to us all. And it is not really possible for those groups to "melt" in the way that the European immigrants did. What happens instead is that an alternative culture is created from the interaction of those groups in the urban setting and a new, dynamic synthesis is effected. As Juan Flores says:

> For this crossing and blending of transmitted colonial cultures is not to be confused with the proverbial "melting pot" of Anglo-American fantasy, nor is it a belated example of "cultural pluralism" as that phrase is commonly used in U.S. social science and public discourse. Though characterized by the plurality and integration of diverse cultures, the process here is not headed toward assimilation with the dominant "core" culture, nor even toward respectful coexistence with it. Rather, the individual and interweaving cultures involved are expressions of histories of conquest, enslavement and forced incorporation at the hands of the prevalent surrounding society. As such, the main thrust in each case is toward self-affirmation and association with other cultures caught up in comparable processes of historical recovery and strategic resistance.[4]

This is where the limitations of a class analysis, uninflected for race, become apparent, for as the living standards of the white working class in this country erode under late capitalism, its members increasingly view these other groups with suspicion or even open hostility. The Reagan Administration's open attack on Affirmative Action is often applauded by white ethnics who are afraid the "minorities" are getting something they are not. But the suspicion and distrust go beyond that kind of rational logic to a more complex underlying fear and intolerance of difference.

When it comes to the Latinos, what makes them vaguely distasteful to some members of the dominant group are those cultural elements they refuse to give up: their spicy foods, their loud Spanish voices, their music. These elements and the cultural resistance they index are the very things which *Trumpets from the Islands of Their Eviction* celebrates.

The Voices Heard

This is a timely book because we are living in a politically fluid historical moment and these poems speak America's other voices. They speak the excluded, the folks whose images rarely appear on television except as the perpetrators of petty crime or as stock figures—undifferentiated "Hispanics." This poetic voice belongs to some of those groups whose cultural forms designers of intelligence tests never use. This poetry gives us privileged access to the dilemmas of a struggling people, dilemmas which never trouble the consumers of mass culture artifacts, for they rarely, if ever, see that other America in plays, books or television programs.

For example, that seamless image of America of which we spoke earlier allows for few eruptions of a disturbing political reality called Puerto Rico. Puerto Rico, and by extension, puertorriqueños are the empire's unmentioned, the colony renamed commonwealth in an Orwellian coup.[5] Puerto Ricans are the excluded who were, ironically, forcibly *included* when the United States unilaterally made them citizens in 1917.[6] Hidden among the media barrage on July fourth is a brief report of an attempted rescue of a Puerto Rican independence fighter from the maximum security prison at Fort Leavenworth.

But puertorriqueños are not the only voices in this book. There are Haitians, Dominicans, United States Blacks, Chicanos, in short, the society's Other, the dispossessed-but-still-with-us who were supposed to fall through the cracks with the advent of Reagan but who continue to struggle, to survive, to overcome. We have here the poor, but not as an undifferentiated entity with an outside and no inside—"the masses." These are not static "images." Perhaps a better metaphor could be taken from the world of the theatre: these people are actors in a drama not of their own making; they are actors who find the script too confining, actors who then rewrite the narrative, or better still, laugh at it.

Mariano Explains Yanqui Colonialism to Judge Collings
Judge: Does the prisoner understand his rights?
Interpreter: ¿Entiende usted sus derechos?
Prisoner: ¡Pa'l carajo!
Interpreter: Yes.

This poetry is oppositional. This is healthy, for it undermines everyday, commonsense notions of an America prosperous and free, an America where, to quote Jimmy Cliff, "you can make it if you really want." This country's favorite mirror image, its collective myth, is now somewhat eroded but the success stories still abound. In the face of governmental wrongdoing and congressional cowardice, in the face of collective alienation and anomie, the multiplicity of discourses on America's greatness generated today have a certain shrillness, an edge of hysteria to them, but they are still produced and produced and produced again.

Amongst the Miss Liberty stories on the tube comes one, delivered in admiring tones, about a person whose apartment on the celebration route will be rented out for the day at a rate of twenty-five thousand dollars—the American dream come true. We turn from that story to:

> . . . Mrs. Alfaro, evicted
> when she trapped ten mice,
> sealed them in plastic sandwich bags
> and gifted them to the landlord;
> like Daniel, the boy stockaded
> in the back of retarded classrooms
> for having no English
> to comfort third-grade teachers;
> like my father thirty-five years ago,
> brown skin darker than the Air Force uniform
> that could not save him, seven days county-jailed
> for refusing the back of a Mississippi bus;
> like the nameless Florida jíbaro
> the grocery stores would not feed
> in spite of the dollars he showed,
> who returned with a machete,
> collected cans from shelves
> and forced the money
> into the clerk's reluctant staring hand.
>   ("Trumpets . . .")

These poems give the lie to the success myth, but they are not poems of despair. They speak resistance in steely Caribbean tones. They are soneos, salsa riffs that speak the music of the barrio and the Island. They resonate with memory traces of the joy one felt as the trumpets and other brass instruments broke into sound the last time one listened to salsa. When las trompetas—metonymic for the orchestra's brass section—make their entry, that joyous metallic celebration takes over the stage and the tropics invade the space with sound. The chain of signification salsa-trumpets-resistance works because, just as the trumpets always return with a blast, so do the evicted, and they do so with the full force of their loud ghetto blasters. They are a metaphoric "return of the repressed," refusing eviction, effectively taking over the space with their music. They will not be denied.

This resistance is sometimes sketched through humor as in the piece entitled "Tiburón":

> East 116th
> and a long red car
> stalled with the hood up
> roaring salsa
> like a prize shark
> mouth yanked open
> and down in the stomach
> the radio
> of the last fisherman
> still tuned
> to his lucky station

The reference is to Rubén Blades' song "Tiburón," an indictment of United States imperialism in Puerto Rico.

Sometimes the resistance is passive:

> *Confession of the Tenant in Apartment #2*
> The landlord's
> beige Fleetwood Cadillac
> died in front of the building,
>
> and I was secretly happy
> that my jumper cables
> didn't work

Sometimes the effect is achieved through color, sound and movement, as in the title poem's final stanza:

> And at the bar two blocks away,
> immigrants with Spanish mouths
> hear trumpets
> from the islands of their eviction.
> The sound scares away devils
> like tropical fish
> darting between the corals.

That last verse captures the bodily sensation of listening to salsa music. We can hear Willie Colón, Ray Barretto, and Rubén Blades jamming together in this poem. We can also visualize the stunning beauty of la Isla.

Literary Tradition

Martín Espada's work belongs to several traditions. First, he writes in English about the immigrant experience, so it can be categorized as United States ethnic literature. Second, as a Puerto Rican, he forms part of a group of writers who refer to themselves and are referred to by critics as Neorican or Nuyorican poets. These are Puerto Rican writers who were born either on the Island or in the United States but who write in English, sometimes using code switching as a discursive strategy.[7] This group includes, among others: Sandra María Esteves, Víctor Hernández Cruz, Tato Laviera and Pedro Pietri. The classic work here is Pedro Pietri's *Puerto Rican Obituary*, a collection of poems first published in 1973.[8] Finally, the Neorican material is itself a sub-category of twentieth century Puerto Rican poetry, the best of which, like Puerto Rican prose writing, has always had a denunciatory function.

Neorican Literature

There are still some linguistic purists among the Island's intellectual elite who deny that this corpus is Puerto Rican literature. They consider it North American ethnic literature, *period*. But this exclusion is the product of a static, one-dimensional view of culture, one which fails to recognize the dynamism of cultural formations and thus mistakenly ignores or marginalizes the work of some very talented Puerto Rican writers. While this attitude is understandable considering Puerto Rico's harsh experience in the schools under United States colonial rule, it is still unfortunately narrow, a perspective that vitiates any possibility of developing a much-needed critical apparatus for analyzing the complex reality that is twentieth-century Puerto Rican society and culture.[9]

This position is unfortunate in social terms as well, for it refuses as foreign the experience of people who, through a series of historico-political circumstances not of their own making, are puertorriqueños de este lado. When we remember that this group constitutes one-third of the Puerto Rican nation, we begin to understand the dimensions of the exclusion. And it is not just that these writers define themselves as Puerto Rican—although ignoring that is at the very least discourtesy—but that their work is Puerto Rican to the core. The themes are the very ones found in the work of Julia de Burgos, Luis Palés Matos, Hugo Margenat and other twentieth-century Puerto Rican poets. No one would dream of excluding these writers from the canon. Nor would they leave out those like Pedro Juan Soto, who wrote in Spanish about the immigrant experience. Puerto Ricans do not give up their national identity just because they change their location *or their language*.[10] Tato Laviera's poem "Nuyorican" captures the combination of pain and false bravado that los de acá feel when excluded by their people back home

>me mandaste a nacer nativo en otras tierras,
>por qué, porqué éramos pobres, ¿verdad?
>porque tú querías vaciarte de tu gente pobre,
>ahora regreso, con un corazón boricua, y tú,
>me desprecias, me miras mal, me atacas mi hablar,
>mientras comes mcdonalds en discotecas americanas,
>. . .
>así que, si tú no me quieres, pues yo tengo
>un puerto rico sabrosísimo en que buscar refugio
>en nueva york, y en muchos otros callejones
>que honran tu presencia . . .[11]

As Efraín Barradas points out, the work of these Neorican poets is thematically continuous with that of nineteenth century Puerto Rican poets.[12] In the Neorican material the Island occupies a central position and not just as a lost origin, although that is also true, as Barradas points out. The puertorriqueños de este lado have a strong bond to the Island, a reality attested to by their peculiarly circular migration pattern. Moreover, the same forces that pushed the Neoricans out have failed the population there:

> *Operation Bootstrap: San Juan, 1985*
> Man with one crutch
> staggering between lanes of traffic
> begging coins
> for the other crutch

At work in this poem is the same dead serious humor that fuels the work of Puerto Rico's best prose writers: it is the humor of a Luis Rafael Sánchez, an Emilio S. Belaval, a César Andreu Iglesias, a Nemesio Canales. It is that humor which undermines authority, the carnival on the steps of the Church, the sudden unmasking of power. It laughs, punctures, lets out the hot air. But the tradition we are speaking of goes back farther, even to Quevedo. It is a peculiarly Hispanic brand of ironic discourse.

United States transfer payments to Puerto Rico were well over $1.5 billion per year in 1979.[13] One possible reading of the crutches in the poem is a metaphor for this aid. The allusion is justified, for social scientists and other critics of the "Puerto Rican Model" often refer to the food stamp program in Puerto Rico in just that way.

José Enamorado Cuesta, an indefatigable independence fighter until his death at the age of eighty-three, would often bemoan the sad fate of a nation reduced to begging for funds before the United States Congress. Once, while driving past an interminable line of people waiting to get their food stamps, he commented to this writer that his people had become una nación de pordioseros—a nation of beggars.[14] Of course, that program, like others in welfare states, contains a hidden contradiction: it is really a welfare program for U.S. investors and transnationals. It guarantees them social stability and a market for their consumer goods. Today Puerto Rico imports more U.S. products per capita than any other country in the world.[15] And it is the food stamp program which makes that possible. It keeps Puerto Rico hobbling along now that its much celebrated "economic miracle" has proven to be slightly less miraculous than planners once thought.

"Brincando el charco—los de acá"

The contemporary Puerto Rican *quehacer* or problematic has one of its best *aproximaciones*—a term the humility of which is missing from all the English equivalents found—in "La guagua aérea" ("The Airbus"), by Luis Rafael Sánchez.[16] In this boundary text between the essay and the short story, Sánchez, with his characteristically acerbic wit, reminds us that Puerto Ricans are up in the air figuratively in the cultural and political sense—yes, once again the status issue—and literally, as they hop back and forth "across the creek." The airbus metaphor in that piece speaks to the way in which los puertorros have appropriated and transformed what was inflicted on them as a people—constant travel back and forth between two places.

This rootlessness appears in Espada's work:

> We have wandered with stuffed bags,
> not staying long enough
> to learn the language.

> ("The Spanish of Our Out Loud Dreams")

But so does that same rice and beans sense of community celebrated by Luis Rafael Sánchez. The poem "Tony Went to the Bodega but He Didn't Buy Anything" is an odyssey through alienation to belonging. After wandering through the cold Anglo parts of his new city where "no one spoke Spanish / (not even the radio),"

> Tony went to the bodega
> but he didn't buy anything:
> he sat by the doorway satisfied
> to watch la gente (people
> island-brown as him)
> crowd in and out,
> hablando español,
> thought: this is beautiful,
> and grinned
> his bodega grin.

> This is a rice and beans
> success story:
> today Tony lives on Tremont Street,
> above the bodega.

The poem is perhaps autobiographical—is Tony a thinly disguised Martín?—it matters not, because the poem speaks of integration of self by means of a bond to a community and as such it is a form of wish-fulfillment. This is especially poignant for those readers who are disconnected from that community. Therein lies its appeal. The poem effects a return to a lost origin, one that is different only in locale from the mythic island which Barradas traces. Although the setting here is the barrio and not the island, the return is complete, wholehearted, and fulfilling. To those of us whose return is always partial, problematic, infused with a desire for wholeness in a fragmented society, the poetic persona's narrative about Tony's plenitude contains all the pleasure of a good fable or fairy tale. The hero is happy at the end for he does go home again.

This, too, is part of the poetic function—to bring that dream material to our awareness, to help us remember or re-member ourselves to a lost wholeness via a re-reading of our dreams. Particularly for people who have been tossed about and repeatedly forced to relocate, the desire for community is a healthy impulse though it is probably wise to recognize it as belonging to the realm of the imaginary.

This connection to a community is effected to a certain extent via the praxis of poetry. And this is poetry whose connection to music and orality has not been severed, these pieces were written to be read aloud, performed, as it were, for the collective. Like the other Neorican poets, Espada reads in community centers, libraries and cafés in Boston, Hartford, Chicago, Los Angeles, and wherever else there is a sizeable Puerto Rican population. The readings take place in a dialogic setting where the audience responds both during and after the readings. The audience is made up of those very people whose lives are the raw material of Espada's poems. They are not an anonymous public nor are they a small one because the devaluation of poetry which has taken place in North America has not been effected among "Hispanics." Hispanic factory workers will bundle up the children and go off to the community center to hear Pedro Pietri, Sandy Esteves or Martín Espada read their work. Instead of being an elite activity, this poetry is part of a broader oral tradition which informs most Latin American cultural products from the Popol Vuh to the sub-genre of testimonial narrative. As such, it is part of a popular culture which challenges the practices of both alienated mass culture and exclusionary elite culture.

Eros

As stated earlier, there is a thematic continuity between Espada's work and that of other Neorican and Island writers. But there is something new as well, a willingness to venture into the dangerous territory of sexuality. In these strangely beautiful pieces, sexuality as a force is coupled with other mysteries such as death and human pain to produce a rhythmic, disturbing effect.

An example of this is the poem "Los Sures." The title refers to South Fourth, Fifth and Sixth Streets, the Williamsburg section of Brooklyn, New York, a Puerto Rican neighborhood with high rates of poverty and crime. The visual and the auditory are combined in the first stanza:

> The bright-color portrait of Jesus jumps
> on South 4th Street plaster
> where the subway train's iron tremor
> startles like the hunger that wakes us,
> night in Los Sures
> shake your black hair down,
> and the night is a woman's darkness.

What accounts for the power of these lines?

Is it that for the New York Puerto Rican community the words "los sures" can be code words for danger? Is it the vivid image of that Jesus—the one with his heart exposed in full color blood, preferably with eyes that open and close? Or is it the poet's use of rhythm? Structured in tension, in an interplay of forces, the poem's dialectic is: hard city fear, danger and darkness acting against the resistance of a people's stubborn will to survive, to overcome, to build. The poetic voice addresses a second person—a woman—whose survival, like that of the collective, depends on a willingness to take on danger. At the same time, it is that danger. As in the free play of desire for the individual subject, for the group, final triumph over the forces of death rests upon overcoming fear. For both, the ally is eros, the libidinal body at play; it is also, when sublimated: music, painting, architecture, indeed all creative work and culture itself. The genius of this poem lies in its attempt to connect eros and community through rhythm. The poem is also a courageous look into those dark forces, which spur us on as a species and threaten us by turns.

Throughout the poem there is a play between outside threat—the street—and inner danger—woman's dark sexuality. An expressionistic second stanza landscapes a deserted street where night is

> . . . the only tenant left,
> night is the face at every window,
> where yellowish heat splashed soot on walls,
> spit a mouthful of glass
> onto South 4th street sidewalk,
> night in Los Sures
> shake your black hair down,
> leaning on the ruined grain of brick.

But in the next stanza the rhythm and tone of the poem shift and it takes a nosedive:

> But the builders have a defiant blueprint,
> the hammer's tap multiplies furious
> as the hands of plena drummers,
> the abandoned church will be a health center,
> the evacuated buildings on South 4th Street
> will shout with the voices of the living . . .

Here, the poetic persona shifts its attention to community praxis, the "defiant blueprint," of those who live there, as the poem tries to tie the music and rhythm of builders' hammers—culture—to the energy that fuels it—eros—a life force over which we ultimately have no control. But although the poet tries to retrieve control of the first stanza:

> night in Los Sures
> shake your black hair down,
> you are a dark woman rising,
> turning hips and heartbeat quick.

it is too late. His attempt to tie in community praxis has marred the poem.

The reason for this formal failure is to be found in an underlying conceptual problem. In *Civilization and Its Discontents*, Sigmund Freud stated that human sexuality and civilization are at odds with one another.[17] So that while the energy or life force that moves us is eros, one cannot simply draw a straight line between that force and the building of community—between " a woman's darkness" and "the hammer's [furious] tap"—because the existence of the one—sexuality—has to be denied or refused to some degree, that is, sublimated, before the other, civilization, building, etc., can take place. Hence the discontent. One of the better-known builders of our era, V. I. Lenin, recognized this truth when he said "We cannot dissipate our energies in sexual debauchery." This impulse to deny the id often informs the discourse of political activists and it indexes an awareness that human desire inevitably affects political praxis.

The problem with this poem lies in an imperfect understanding of a complex problem, the sad fact that libido and culture are in some sense at odds with each other. What is left out or elided here is sexuality's capacity to *both* fuel our work and disrupt our plans. This is what the poem started out to problematize and did not. When the transition in the poem's third stanza breaks the flow and rhythm established in the first two stanzas, it is because the conceptual weakness which underlies the formal break makes the poem difficult, obscure; it makes it a different poem. It is now *political* in the simple sense of the word. It is self-consciously *about* "the community" and its struggle, but seen now from the outside. This is disappointing because the first two stanzas promised us an inside view.

It is unfortunate that the poem's ambitious goal fails to materialize, but Espada is right to work with this material. When it comes to understanding the human psyche, the poets have always had the advantage. Freud recognized this when he stated that they, not he, had discovered the unconscious. Fredric Jameson goes so far as to call for a new science to apprehend the human subject.

> The libidinal body, as a field and instrument of perception all at once, cannot but be self-indulgent. . . . To discipline it, to give it the proper tasks and ask it to repress its other random impulses, is at once to limit its effectiveness, or, even worse, to damage it irretrievably. Lazy, shot through with fits of boredom or enthusiasm, reading the world and its texts with nausea or with *jouissance*, listening for the fainter vibrations of a sensorium largely numbed by civilization and rationalization, sensitive to the messages of throbs too immediate, too recognizable as pain or pleasure—maybe all this is not to be described as self-indulgence after all. Maybe it requires a discipline and a responsiveness of a rare yet different sort, something like free association (outsmarting the instant defenses of the ego or the rationalizing intellect) or boating, sensing and riding with a minimal current.

Maybe indeed the deeper subject is here: not "pleasure" . . . but
the libidinal body itself, and *its* peculiar politics, which may well
move in a realm largely beyond the "pleasurable" in that narrow,
culinary, bourgeois sense.[18]

It is anybody's guess why Espada shifted his attention from
the dark force of sexuality to the more acceptable theme of
community building, especially since in his earlier collection he
showed his mastery in handling fire. In "Mrs. Báez Serves Cof-
fee on the Third Floor" there is, for fire, an effect on the reader
similar to the one we wish he had explored for sexuality.

> It hunches
> with a brittle black spine
> where they poured
> gasoline on the stairs
> and the bannister
> and burnt it.
>
> The fire went running
> down the steps,
> a naked lunatic,
> calling the names
> of the neighbors,
> cackling in the hall.
>
>   ("Mrs. Báez Serves Coffee . . . ")[19]

In both poems the force unleashed has an unexpected, crazy
dimension. It is a wild card that—like fire, like a woman's sexual-
ity—takes on life suddenly and becomes a threat.

Of course, the opposition between fire and community praxis
is clearer than that between eros and building, but Espada would
do well to rework "Los Sures" to its full potential.

The first poem of the collection, "The Spanish of Our Out-
Loud Dreams," works with eros as well, except that this time it
has a healing function. The poetic persona's lover is a woman
whose father is dying in a hospital. The poetic voice invokes eros
to comfort both the woman and her father. First he tries to
soothe her pain with his hands:

> My hand slipped through the night-thicket
> of your hair,
> as if the circling of my fingers
> could give you rest.

When that fails, the voice moves to identify with the pain of the dying father. He thinks of the comfort which the daughter's passion has afforded him and, in his desire to help the dying man, he transforms this passion into a salve, a space of safety to share:

> Let him sleep
> where I slept:
> shining in your passionate blackness,
> the vigil of your shimmering gaze.

In taking up eros, Espada is in the company of some of the best contemporary Chicano poets. Two of these, Pat Mora and Juan Felipe Herrera, write of eros from different vantage points. While Pat Mora's poetic persona is southwestern, female and firmly grounded in nature, Juan Felipe Herrera's is an urban exile. Two examples will suffice to illustrate this new thematic opening now taking place in Chicano literature. First Mora:

> *Unrefined*
>
> The desert is no lady.
> She screams at the spring sky,
> dances with her skirts high,
> kicks sand, flings tumbleweeds,
> digs her nails into all flesh.
> Her unveiled lust fascinates the sun.[20]

and Herrera:

> *Children of Space*
>
> I
>
> On Valencia Street the playground aches. Children float through parking lots riddled with the screams of distant throats. Daughter-hands toss the toy over the clouds; invisible. The mother in apartment G gazes, not inhaling. The father coils the fingers around transparent shoulders in the air. Slowly, they undress. Only the stains of the assassinations remain on their bodies. They do not speak now. They cannot speak. Willingly, they have cut something inside. Vowels bleed across the sheets.
>
> II
>
> They enter windows. They exit through small openings. Even their bones are changing. Soon, they will be unable to walk. The two will end in a stance, nude; one pressed against the toilet towel

rack, the mirror speckled with images of rapid hands wet. The other hits each fist against the living room wall; please me/leave me.

III

In the sunlight the children rotate in soundless collisions,
                                                    beyond the rented
        structures
            into an infinite system of undecipherable signs.[21]

Pinball Between Madhouses

In this third and final section of the book, Espada inscribes another group of "others" whose exclusion has nothing to do with ethnicity or race. They are outside because they cannot perform according to society's codes. They are the insane, the criminal, the poor, the illiterate. Their stories, too, have been elided, ignored or erased by a highly codified society that rejects those who fail to abide by its rules.

Music plays a key role here as well. There are references in almost every poem to some type of music: gospel music, ragtime, jazz, Gregorian chants, salsa, even polka music. But ubiquitous as music is in the first section of the book, in this section its role is more varied. Note, for example, the gradual shift in the symbolic value of the polka between the third verse and the final verse in the following poem:

> *The Policeman's Ball*
>
> It was
> a policeman's ball,
> old-timey cop stomp
> polka kept the beat
> with a boot blood-spotted
> and a hand that clapped,
> so that after the dance
> the suspect couldn't
> snap his fingers

That music is anything but humorous. Compare it with the Gregorian chant in "Eight Hundred A.D. On the Ward": "An observation patient / wailing through / the night watchman's sleep / is only remembering / a Gregorian chant / from the monastery / he visits in dreams."

The well-wrought "Majeski Plays the Saxophone" is a study in

contrasts between the external "image" of a sociopath—so de-
fined by doctors and social workers—and the saxophone player's
connection to his instrument: "devils tattooed on his arms, /
headshaking overgrown hair and beard / with the murmur of the
trembled horn, / bodyrocking to saxophone's / drugged confes-
sion."

Music is also here on a formal level in the rhythmic control of
verses like:

> All day bending
> like something storm-broken
> and left to sway,
> dream scarecrows
> with stiff hands picking.
> Ten hours gone.
>
> ("Leo Blue's and the Tiger Rose")

The best poems here are crisp, their imagery sharp, almost
harsh. Note, for example, the cold fluorescence of the scene in a
mental hospital, a setting whose sterility matches the mental
sterility induced by the drugs the institution feeds its patients:

> ### Drugs in the Forehead
>
> Iron doors, windows sunken and repeating themselves
> in sterilized corridors, fluorescent lights
> and mopped floors spotted in a dream state,
> scrubfleshed hand dutifully keeping the logbook;
> dayroom, used furniture in the corner,
> television's image greying and dumb,
> a coffee cup, the ward tilted to the angle
> of slouched men, between every bored cigarette
> a face with drugs in the forehead.

Trumpets from the Islands of Their Eviction is a self-confident
look from the margins, a critique of the so-called center whose
values must not only be examined but changed.

UNIVERSITY OF IOWA
OCTOBER 1986

Notes

¹ Martín Espada, *The Immigrant Iceboy's Bolero*, (Natick, MA: Cordillera Press, 1984).

² Pedro Pietri, *Puerto Rican Obituary* (New York: Monthly Review Press, 1973), p. 10.

³ "'Qué assimilated, brother, yo soy asimilao': the Structuring of Puerto Rican Identity in the U.S." *Journal of Ethnic Studies* 13:3 (1985), 1-16.

⁴ Ibid., 3-4.

⁵ The "Estado Libre Asociado," established in 1952, legitimized U.S. political control of the Island. Significantly, the term used in English for Puerto Rico's sui generis status is "commonwealth."

⁶ The reference is to the 1917 law known as the Jones Act, whereby Puerto Rican citizenship was unilaterally abolished by the U.S. Congress and Puerto Ricans were made U.S. citizens.

⁷ Code switching is the alternating use of two languages or two language varieties in one utterance. It is used effectively as a poetic device by both Chicano and Puerto Rican writers. For a sensitive analysis of this strategy, see Guadalupe Valdés Fallis, "Code-Switching in Bilingual Chicano Poetry," *Hispania* 59, 4 (Dec. 1976), 877-886.

⁸ See note 2.

⁹ The debate over which language should be used as a teaching medium in the Island's public schools is a long and bitter chapter in Puerto Rico's history. It is clearly tied to the status issue and to political events on the island. In the first part of the century, the goal of educational policymakers was to "Americanize" the Puerto Rican child by using English as the language of instruction, with Spanish taught as a separate subject. The policy was enunciated in 1903, went into effect in 1905 and, according to Charles F. Reid, of Columbia University's Teacher's College, "in 1909 Commissioner Edwin G. Dexter carried the . . . policy to . . . the height of absurdity by providing in the first grade, for the teaching of the mechanics of reading in English, but not in Spanish." This in a country that had been speaking Spanish for 400 years. See, Charles F. Reid, "Education in the Territories and Outlying Possessions," in *Teachers College Contributions to Education* (New York: Columbia University Press, 1941), p. 273. For a complete history and analysis of the language issue and the Puerto Rican people's struggle to learn in their own language, see: Aída Negrón de Montilla, *Americanization in Puerto Rico and the Public School System—1900–1930* (Río Piedras: Editorial Edil, 1972); and Nilita Vientós Gastón, "El tribunal supremo de Puerto Rico y el problema de la lengua," *Casa de las Américas* 70 (1972), 64-72.

¹⁰ The Chicano experience is instructive here. Cultural identity for Chicanos is not eroded even as they become monolingual English speakers. And while some critics such as Manuel Maldonado-Denis cite the experience of the Chicanos in tones of horror and sadness for the

consumption of a Puerto Rican reading public, this experience can also be read as a fine example of cultural resistance. See Manuel Maldonado-Denis, *Puerto Rico y Estados Unidos: emigración y colonialismo* (México, D.F.: Siglo XXI, 1976). See especially pp. 123-154. Juan Flores' work (see esp. note 4), among others', represents a different view, one which goes a long way toward changing the static view of the older critics.

[11] Tato Laviera, "Nuyorican," *AmeRícan* (Houston: Arte Público Press, 1979), p. 53.

[12] Efraín Barradas, "De lejos en sueños verla . . . ," *Revista Chicano-Riqueña* VII, 3 (verano 1979), pp. 46-56. See also "Puerto Rico acá, Puerto Rico allá," *Revista Chicano-Riqueña* VIII, 2 (primavera 1980), pp. 43-49.

[13] *NACLA Report on the Americas* XV, 2 (March-April 1981), introductory page (not numbered) of special issue on Puerto Rico entitled "Puerto Rico—End of Autonomy."

[14] Personal communication with the author, San Juan, Puerto Rico, May 1975.

[15] *NACLA*, see note 13.

[16] Luis Rafael Sánchez, "The Airbus" (translation of "La guagua aérea"), tr. Diana Vélez, *The Village Voice*, XXIX, 5 (Jan. 31, 1984), pp. 39-43.

[17] S. Freud, *Civilization and Its Discontents*, tr. James Strachey (New York: Norton, 1961).

[18] Fredric Jameson, "Pleasure: A Political Issue," *Formations of Pleasure* (London: Routledge and Kegan Paul, 1983), p. 9.

[19] Espada, "Mrs. Báez . . ." in *The Immigrant Iceboy's Bolero*.

[20] Pat Mora, *Chants* (Houston: Arte Público Press, 1984), p. 8.

[21] Juan Felipe Herrera, *Exiles of Desire* (Houston: Arte Público Press, 1985), p. 8.

AUTHOR'S BIBLIOGRAPHY

Previous Book

The Immigrant Iceboy's Bolero. Madison, WI: Ghost Pony Press, 1982; reprinted by
Cordillera Press, Natick, MA, 1983; reprinted by Waterfront Press, Maple-
wood, NJ, 1986.

Poems in Anthologies

"Waiting for the Cops." In *Hispanics in the United States: An Anthology of Creative
Literature, Vol. II.* Ed. Gary Keller and Francisco Jiménez. Ypsilanti, MI:
Bilingual Press, 1982, p. 182.

"Pinball Between Madhouses," "The Immigrant Iceboy's Bolero," and "Adolfo
and Lucia." In *Wire in the Blood: Political Poems From Madison, Wisconsin.* Ed.
Dennis Trudell. Madison, WI: Abraxas Press, 1982, pp. 3-5, 29-31.

"Los Sures," "Puerto Rican Autopsy," "Heart of Hunger," "The Immigrant Ice-
boy's Bolero," and "Adolfo and Lucia." In *A Confluence of Colors: The First
Anthology of Wisconsin Minority Poets.* Madison, WI: Blue Reed Arts Press,
1985, pp. 63-68. "Los Sures" rpt. in this volume.

"Waiting for the Cops." In *Editor's Choice II: Fiction, Poetry and Art From the U.S.
Small Press.* Ed. Morty Sklar and Mary Biggs. Iowa City, IA: The Spirit That
Moves Us Press, 1987.

Poems in Periodicals

"Mrs. Báez Serves Coffee on the Third Floor." *Abraxas* (Madison, WI), #23/24,
October 1981, pp. 21-23.

"Majeski Plays the Saxophone," "Unfinished Business." *Jump River Review* (Pren-
tice, WI), #11, Spring 1982, pp. 18-19, 60.

"Manuel Is Quiet Sometimes." *Abraxas* (Madison, WI), #25/26, May 1982, pp. 78-
79. Rpt. in this volume.

"Cordillera," "One Night Stand in the Milk of an Industrial Moon." *Madison
Review* (Madison, WI), Vol. 4, No. 1, Winter 1982, pp. 39-41.

"The Firing Squad is Singing in Chile," "Tato Hates the New York Yankees," and
"Power." *Bilingual Review/Revista Bilingüe* (Ypsilanti, MI), Vol. 9, No. 2, May-
August 1982, pp. 156-160. "The Firing Squad is Singing in Chile" rpt. in this
volume.

"Leo Blue's and the Tiger Rose." *Greenfield Review* (Greenfield Center, NY), Vol. 12, Nos. 1 and 2, Summer/Fall 1984, pp. 185-186. Rpt. in this volume.

"The Jeep Driver," "Again the Mercenaries: Atlantic Coast of Nicaragua, 4th of July 1982," and "David Leaves the Saints for Paterson." *Revista Chicano-Riqueña* (Houston, TX), Vol. 7, No. 2, Summer 1984, pp. 32-35. All rpt. in this volume.

"The Spanish of Our Out-Loud Dreams" and "La tormenta." *Imagine: International Chicano Poetry Journal* (Boston, MA), Vol. 1, No. 2, Winter 1984, pp. 141-143. Both rpt. in this volume.

"Trumpets From the Islands of Their Eviction." *Bloomsbury Review* (Denver, CO), Vol. 5, No. 7, April 1985, p. 12. Rpt. in this volume.

"Voodoo Cucumbers" and "Tiburón." *Pinchpenny* (Sacramento, CA), Vol. 6, No. 1, April 1985, pp. 26-27. Both rpt. in this volume.

"Mariano Explains Yanqui Colonialism to Judge Collings," "Inmate Torres Sings Waiting for the Parole Board," and "Job Search Got Us Down." *Tonantzin* (San Antonio, TX), Vol. 3, No. 1, November 1985, p. 10. All rpt. in this volume.

"The Immigrant Iceboy's Bolero" and "Haiku Bailando." *Centro de Estudios Puertorriqueños Newsletter* (New York, NY), June 1986, pp. 16-17.

"Grito for Nicaragua" and "Operation Bootstrap: San Juan, 1985." *Hanging Loose* (Brooklyn, NY), #49, September 1986, p. 12. Both rpt. in this volume.

Other Publications

Editor:
"Ten Latino Poets," Latino Poetry Supplement to *Hanging Loose*, #52, Summer 1987.

Article:
"Documentaries and Declamadores: Puerto Rican Poetry in the United States." *A Gift of Tongues*. Ed. Kathleen Agüero and Marie Harris. Athens, GA: University of Georgia Press, 1987.

Reviews and Criticism

Clark, Rod. Review of *The Immigrant Iceboy's Bolero*, in *City Lights*, November 19-December 2, 1982, pp. 5, 12.

Keller, Gary. Mention of *The Immigrant Iceboy's Bolero*, in "Materials Received," *Bilingual Review/Revista Bilingüe*, Vol. 9, No. 3, September-December 1982, p. 280.

Review of *The Immigrant Iceboy's Bolero*, in "Three New Books by Hispanic Poets," *Hispanic Arts News*, November-December 1984, p. 3.

González, Ray. Mention of *The Immigrant Iceboy's Bolero*, in "Bibliophile: Poetry," *Bloomsbury Review*, Vol. 5, No. 4, January 1985, p. 21.

Black, Robert. Review of *The Immigrant Iceboy's Bolero*, in "Literature and Language: Reviews, *Lector*, Vol 3, No. 4, Spring 1985.

García, Edward. Review of *The Immigrant Iceboy's Bolero*, in "Reviews," *Revista Chicano-Riqueña*, Vol. 13, No. 2, Summer 1985, pp. 72-74.

Flores, Juan. Review of *The Immigrant Iceboy's Bolero*, in *Centro de Estudios Puertorri-queños Newsletter*, June 1986, p. 15.

Aparicio, Frances. Review of *The Immigrant Iceboy's Bolero*, in *Imagine: International Chicano Poetry Journal*, Vol. 2, No. 2, Summer 1986.

Cortina, Rodolfo. Mention of Martín Espada in "Hispanic-American Poetry in Wisconsin." In *A Confluence of Colors*. Ed. Angela Lobo-Cobb. Madison, WI: Blue Reed Arts Press, 1984.